Strength for the Sadness

Zeta Combs Davidson

ISBN: 978-0-578-75849-7

Independently Published by Barker/Haulman Media

Printed and bound in the United States of America

Table of Contents

Introduction

Wherever you are in your need for strength, thank you for joining me. Let's pursue this small space of peace.

You may be at the point where you don't want to leave your house. The day goes pretty well, but when you turn into your driveway grief washes over you. You may be at some other point in your grief process. No one knows exactly how you feel even if they say they do.

Sadness from grief is what we receive from loving another well. You may feel that no one else has ever felt like you do. Your sadness is newer and keener. You may be at the point it is difficult to say much.

My experience found left-brained me not able to concentrate. As I tried to read my Bible, the words blurred on the page. I just needed to 'get through' the day. With these two realities in mind, I've penned a month's worth of devotions that helped me 'put one foot in front of the other.' These daily devotions are short. I know from experience you may not want or be able to concentrate for long. I hope each highlights an idea or two to 'keep you going.'

Imagine we are having a cup of coffee at your table or mine. My journey started some years ago. Although I have always known I might walk this path, I didn't know it would start on that August 21, the day my husband and best friend, Don, died after a three-year struggle with cancer. I found grieving to be hard work—some of the most difficult of my life.

Your loss may be a dear friend or a different family member. Your journey may be much like mine or it may be completely different. I can say only what helped me. I trust you will be encouraged.

Read only one devotion a day and concentrate on any phrase that will help you. Choose what's best for you. Each day includes a Scripture verse that encouraged me. I hope that is true for you. There is space for your thoughts.

Although your life will never be the same, it can and will go on. You will look back to see blessings now and in days ahead. God has plans for each of us we know nothing about.

This is your time to grieve. I pray God's strength for your sadness. ~ *Zeta*

Never Forget

God showed us how much he loved us by sending his only Son into the world so that we might have eternal life through him. John 4: 9 (NLT)

"How are you doing?" That's the question I heard most often. Has the same been true for you since your loved one passed?

Yes, I often thought–How am I doing?

I knew I could lie and say, "Fine."

When did I start saying? "Doing as well as I can . . .".

Three weeks after a person's death, acquaintances I'd meet on the street would forget.

Whether three weeks, three years or thirty years, you will never forget. No one told me about forcing myself out of bed each morning, forcing myself to shower and dress. I found an inner strength I never knew I had. With hardly realizing it, I knew someone was praying for me. Even when I hesitated to pray, I managed to say, "Thank you, Lord."

Yes, some said, "I know how you feel." Each of us are individuals. No one can know exactly how we feel.

I remember appreciating those who said, "I've been there and I'm sorry."

If we were together today, I'd just say, "What happened?" Even when friends avoided the subject, I needed to talk. All I needed was a listener to the details. My hope continues that these kinds of friends are there and will continue to be there for you.

Also, I later so appreciated the friend who shared, "If at all possible, make funeral arrangements ahead of time." Yes, when you can think more clearly. Plus costs may be less by many dollars.

If I had waited, my emotions might have gotten the best of me when I was told, "I know you will want this and this for your loved one."

My reaction, "No my loved one would never want a lavish display nor me saddled with a large debt."

No, I'll never forget. No, you will never forget. Your experience has been and will be different from mine–yet, our happenings may also be eerily the same.

Dear God, you know the pain. A good friend's death caused you to weep. Amen.

Notes

Your Current Need

God replied, "I AM THE ONE WHO ALWAYS IS." Exodus 3:14a (NLT)

How many days has it been since you stood graveside? How many months? How many years? No doubt, you will recall within seconds the exact time, date and place.

Our relationship with those whom God sent to be an intimate part of our lives continues in thoughts, happenings and dates on calendars.

How would you fill in the blank when God quietly speaks to you today?

"I AM_____."

What is your *real* need today? Would you like a bit less emotional pain of separation? Would you like less loneliness?

God says, "Fill in the blank with your need and I will supply it." Just for today, you and I may see this new life we did not order in a more positive way.

Dear God, not for what we want, but for what we need, you say,
"*I am_____" and invite us to fill in the blank. Thank you. Amen.*

Personal thoughts

_____

_____

_____

_____

_____

_____

_____

_____

Why Celebrate?

And I am convinced that nothing can ever separate us from Christ's love.
Death can't . . . Romans 8:38a (NLT)

One morning I felt overwhelmed. My world seemed so empty. My body was so physically tired all I wanted to do was sleep. Yes, I wished I could wake up and everything would be all right.

After staring into space for who knows how long, my eyes focused on the iron letters atop my sideboard–connected letters spelling Celebrate. Although they been there a couple of years, I ignored them during my time of grief. Somehow that morning, my attention would not leave them. I forced myself to think–*What do I have to celebrate?* My family with their hugs, their calls, their continual caring. My health–as my coronary physician reported he had not seen a healthier heart this year. My friends–the church and its balcony overflowed at the funeral. My church family–encircling our house to pray for Don's healing–even though it did not happen in this life.

Now I comfort others who face the loss of close relationships. Private grief takes so many forms and happens when we least expect it: a touch, a smell, a memory, a sight.

There is no right way or wrong way to grieve. Grief continues as a very personal thing. Even though others seem to forget in just a few weeks, we may never get over it, but we can celebrate what is good.

Dear God, thank you for showing me to celebrate, even in the midst of grief.
Amen.

No One Knows

God blesses the people who patiently endure testing.
Afterward they will receive the crown of life. James 1:12a (NLT)

The death of Don produced one of the greatest tests of my entire life. Someone said to me, "I know exactly how you feel." No, no one knows exactly how any of us feel. I tried to keep in mind that person meant only to console.

I finally learned words to replace blurting, "No, you don't." I started answering with a question.

In the kindest voice, my reply became, "What makes you say that?" Then I made a real effort to listen and find some part of their response I could agree with.

Then I quietly spoke, "What I've also learned is ...." I shared whatever feelings I could muster.

Most often, I appreciated someone just saying, "What happened?" It helped me to verbalize what was inside–a need to just talk.

Without a doubt, someone who says, "I know just how you feel" would not be using the phrase unless they also experienced deep sadness.

Maybe Max Lucado[1] had it right when he said, "You don't get over this. With God's help, you will get through this."

Dear God, allow me to listen, to help and realize deep sadness comes to all of us.
Amen.

Reaction _____

_____

_____

_____

_____

My Weakness—God's Strength

My grace is enough: it's all you need. My strength comes into its own in your weakness. 2 Corinthians 12:9 (MSG)

Following my husband's death, each decision seemed insurmountable, almost catastrophic. I kept thinking, *What I do about…?* Fill in the blank with anything. I spent considerable time feeling overwhelmed.

My natural response was, *I can't go on.*

Although this next comment may be upsetting, the truth is we can and will do both. Few decisions must be made at a minute's notice. Most can be postponed a day, a week and some indefinitely. One exercise that strengthened me, in retrospect, was to draw a circle on paper, then ask myself, "What things are in my circle of control this minute…this day?"

The realization finally sunk in, God was saying, "When you feel weakest, I am strongest." Right now, it may be difficult for you to focus on anything you try to read. Even reading the Bible may be the last thing you are able to do.

In Second Corinthians 12:10, Paul was not referring to grieving a death. He was referring to grieving his handicap. We may feel handicapped by grief. I found help by saying over and over each day, "God's grace is mine. My weakness is turned into strength by Him."

Dear Lord, Your grace is mine this moment. Your grace will be enough. Let me access my circle of control to complete what is necessary today. Amen

Circle of control today _____

_____

_____

_____

_____

_____

Strength and Peace

The Lord gives His people strength; the Lord blesses His people with peace.
Psalm 29:1 (NLT)

I rediscovered one simple truth. After a family member or close friend dies, most people will remember to offer condolences for three weeks.

But reality discovers you are just beginning to spend time in some stage of your grief. Some grievers will still be in shock after three weeks. Some will have more than overwhelming sadness. Some will have even progressed to anger.

I could navigate the day-to-day world with only some difficulty. Then I would get in my car to drive home, and grief would encompass me. Sometimes there were oceans of tears–other times, quiet sobbing. If I could keep myself from thinking too much, I might be composed by the time I got home. I was taught the-sadness breeds-sadness effect.

One surprising thing was that even though I was alone, I never felt lonely. That's when this verse in Psalm 29 became a reality. Both friends and acquaintances reminded me I was still on their prayer list–even after the usual three weeks. My blessing of peace was God's answer to their prayers for my need.

Oh Lord, thank you for the emotional strength You give mercifully during our grieving journey.

Help us to realize only You give true peace. Amen

Difficulties _____

_____

_____

_____

_____

_____

Give Yourself a Break

"…Don't feel bad. The joy of God is your strength!" Nehemiah 8:10b (MSG)

Look outside with me. Is the sun shining? Recall that childhood song, "Heavenly sunshine, heavenly sunshine, flooding my soul with glory divine."

Whatever I have to do, I tell myself, "God wants you to find some sunshine of joy in this day." For instance, today I stopped to admire rosebush blooms and noted that robin babies in the nest on the grapevine wreath. Their mouths open, waiting for mother bird to bring a worm.

"Seems like we walk with one foot in grief and the other in an altered state. Surreal. Numb. Recreating oneself. The wildest times of grief are settled by God's arms of comfort and love. What a strange journey," posted my widow friend, Debbie Davis, on FaceBook. Perhaps this is the day for us to give ourselves a hug.

This may be just day to give yourself a break. My pastor says, "God calls it grace."

To regain focus, I jotted down three things I wanted to accomplish the next day, then by wrote three things I was grateful for. My bookshelf boasts four of these 6" x 8" hardbacks filled with my words. It became a contest to see how many things I could be thankful for before I repeated.

Dear Lord, my life is in a state of confusion today. Help me order the steps of today's journey so I may find joy and be grateful. Amen.

Three things to accomplish _____

_____

_____

Three things to be grateful for _____

_____

_____

_____

God Feels Our Pain

Give thanks in all circumstances, for this is God's will for you...
1 Thessalonians 5:18 (NIV)

One day I found myself at wit's end, wondering, "If God loves me so much, how could He have allowed my loved one to die?"

Maybe you haven't been thinking of God because you just can't think, let alone consider being thankful in all things. From the recesses of my mind comes the thought *God is closer than the air we breathe.* Let me remind myself and include you—God has said He will never leave us nor forsake us.

Perhaps it doesn't matter that our pain has caused us to push God away—even to ignore His existence. Why don't I remember the cross? Any pain I feel, He has already felt. Do I think within the limits of my human mind that God did not suffer when He allowed His only son, Jesus, to be nailed to the cross and experience a humiliating death?

In reality I know, we can push God away physically and emotionally. He remains ready to be welcomed in our hearts and lives to console our skeptical souls.

Thanking God for where I found myself seemed impossible. Because of this verse from 1 Thessalonians, I did it anyway. I told Him, "God, my worst fears are now my reality."

Time passed. Then I could concentrate enough to again realize we cannot experience any thought, emotion or circumstance that He does not know.

Encouraging Words: I may not feel like thanking God, but I'll do it anyway.
I'll seek to draw as close as I can to God even when silently screaming
with suffering.

Gaining Strength

...For you have not passed this way before. Joshua 3:4b (NASB)

No matter how death intruded on your life, whether from a car wreck, long-lived life, cancer or some other way, the one you loved so much is gone.

There is satisfaction that any suffering is over. If your loved one was a believer, his soul is now in heaven with God. Although neither of us may see this occurrence as fair, I continue to learn that those of us left behind must understand death for its reality. We can accept the comfort others offer and also the comfort only God can bring.

Family, friends and acquaintances tried to help me by giving advice. After a few days, I learned to say "Thank you. I'll consider it." My nearest neighbors avoided coming over. Later they admitted, "We did not know what to say or do."

I received condolences from those I never thought I would hear from. At the same time, people I thought I would hear from distanced themselves. One couple who were close friends, came every evening that last week and simply sat with me. For the first time, I realized everyone grieves in his or her own way.

You and I are not the only ones who are deeply saddened. The most helpful were good friends who acknowledged, "I don't know how you feel, but I love and care for you."

Some decisions had to be made. I found, as you may, strength I didn't know was present. My best guess as to its source? God knew the kind of strength I now needed. When I thought, *I cannot go on–I'm sure it was the Holy Spirit who urged me; thank God for His presence and power.*

Dear God, this time of desperately deep sadness seems more than I can bear. Thank You for strength and the presence of mind that comes from You. Amen.

Helpful happenings_____

_____

_____

_____

Happenings not at all helpful_____

_____

_____

_____

_____

_____

Force Yourself a Bit

Come near to God and he will come near to you. Grieve, mourn...
James 4:8a & 9a (NIV)

Is this the day for you to be angry? Angry--at God, that is. While it may not be the first day, it may also not be the last. Verbally, I had to say out loud, "Calm yourself."

A friend shared with me, "God can take it." She gently asked if I'd ever given God a reason to be disgruntled with me. I knew the answer.

The emotional hurt was the kind where I wanted someone to blame. As my friend said, "It's okay, if you are blaming God, He can take it, He will even leave you alone if you like."

Then remembered a teaching learned at a young age--God always loves me no matter what. Somewhere in the back of my mind, the old hymn sang "...He's waiting and watching for you and for me."

On numerous days, I was angry with God. Then I recalled, "God can take whatever you wish to say to Him or whatever feelings you may have toward Him." Jesus died on the cross, a wicked and painful death. Whatever I was feeling, He had felt worse pain.

The question became, "Zeta, what are you going to do with your pain?"

My daughter, Paige–grieving in her own way–suggested one way to handle painful depressing emotions, "What are you grateful for right now, Mom? What are three blessings you can thank God for today in the midst of this misery?" Some days I answered on note paper, some days in a spiral notebook, other days I used a journal. As I forced myself to center on three each day, with none being renamed a second time, I found this became a good way to not feel sorry for myself.

Notice, I didn't say, "Don't feel sorry for yourself." It is normal to care about your feelings. I tried not to allow myself to stay in that frame of mind for more than an hour. While walking in my neighborhood, I felt a breeze blowing across my face. Could this be the gentle way God was feeling toward me? No anger, just sweet compassion.

Dear God, I'm so angry with You, I feel like biting a spike in two.
I'm questioning whether You know how sad I really am.
Please show me something to be grateful for today. Amen

Thoughts on anger toward God _____

_____

_____

_____

_____

Handling painful depressing emotions_____

_____

_____

_____

_____

Is This Normal?

"Does Job fear God for nothing?" Satan replied, "Have you not put a hedge around him...?" Job 1:9-10a (NIV)

At least once I allowed myself to think, "If God cared enough, this grief might not be happening." Perhaps you never thought you could hurt emotionally this much.

Yes, I did know about the story of Job. Even then, God told Satan, "You can do anything to Job, but you cannot lay a hand on Job himself." As the chapters continued, I read what happened to this wonderful follower of God—Job....

Job lost everyone in his immediate family, including his wife.

I know you must be in agreement when I say, "Death of a family member hurts so much." In my case, I missed conversations the most. Whatever has happened in your family, I doubt it compares to Job's grief. In fact, the Bible states that in Job's case, his hurt was so intense he wished he had never been born.

My mother always said, "When you feel you've been dealt your worst blow, look around. You can always find someone with more needs than you." Even when I least wanted to follow Mom's advice, I knew it to be true. You didn't think you could hurt emotionally this much, did you? Even those times when I didn't want to look beyond myself, I learned later it was totally normal.

Oh Lord, how can I endure this hurt I feel? I'm trying, Lord, but everything I see gives reminders. Yes, Lord, is it okay just to try when I don't feel normal? Amen.

First Year Pain

Peace, I leave with you; My peace I give to you...Do not let your hearts be troubled and do not be afraid. John 14:27 (NIV)

My daughter, Paige, worded it best when she said, "If my Dad hadn't been so sick for so long, I could never have stood it." Lurking on the edges of my thought patterns numerous times, I wondered why would a good God permit such suffering?

Sometimes that first year, it took all of my emotional strength not to fall into a trap of unbelief, "Am I sure God is truly good?" I could not concentrate long enough to read Scripture when that had been my daily habit. I relied on verses or parts of verses that had been committed to memory. I literally made myself read one verse a day from a devotional book.

"I will never leave you nor forsake you," was one day's verse with its reference, Joshua 1:5b (NIV). I remember getting up from the blue chair in my living room and walking into my bedroom to look in the full-length mirror. My reflection showed that on the outside, my appearance and dress were no different than prior to Don's death.

But on the inside, I was silently shrieking, "There is nothing fair about all this suffering and grief." As days became weeks and weeks became months, I later realized how God had been with the one suffering cancer. God was also with my family and me in our grief.

Lord God, help me always remember the pain You experienced
when Your Son lived on earth.
He lived a blameless life, then was beaten and crucified.
You have experienced my pain.
You are truly good. Amen.

Drawers of Memories

On us who live in the dark shadow of death, God's light will shine to guide us into a path of peace. Luke 1:79 (CEV)

Wooden sideboard or cabinet, I don't know what they are really called. I do know they have at least twenty-one drawers, some painted different colors. One for sale keeps showing up on the sidebar of my computer.

One day I considered, if this were a grief cabinet, each of its multiple drawers could represent a different memory tucked inside. If all the drawers were opened at once, grief overwhelmed.

But if just one was opened, perhaps while I was driving–a random sight or sign struck my memory–I shed a tear and wiped it away.

If one or more of the drawers were left open, I might go a whole day with certain memories just below the surface of all my thoughts.

Over time, it has grown easier for most all the drawers of memories to remain closed. But the memories are always there–reminders of the person for whom I cared so much.

Occasionally, I would straighten a drawer or two. During these times, God helped me think more realistically of the one I was mourning–a person who loved and served Him, but who was also human with faults and imperfections.

Even the color of each drawer began to serve as a reminder. Painted blue? Those are the serene times. Yellow? The sunny, good and happy times. The red drawers? When our lives were halted by challenges or illness. Then there were the green drawers–our times of growth and gladness.

Neither you nor I may have this actual piece of furniture. I have only a chest of drawers in my home. Is it fair to think it is normal to open one of the drawers of our memories, allow grief to be real and then gently close the drawer?

Dear God some days my life is so muddled by the sadness, it feels as if every drawer in my chest is open with memories spilling out. Help me to savor the memories–but not too long. Amen.

Drawers of memory to open _____

_____

_____

_____

_____

_____

_____

_____

_____

_____

_____

_____

When Will We Know?

No eye has seen, no mind has conceived what God has prepared for those who love him. 1 Corinthians 2:9 (NIV)

My interest peaked as I sat at a recent Celebration of Life service. Pastor Don Wideman shared a question the gentleman who had been in Hospice had asked, "What will it be like in heaven. Will we know what is happening to those loved ones we left?"

I moved to the edge of my seat anticipating how the pastor would respond. A hush came over the crowd. Each wanted to know the answer to those questions. Wideman, a retired pastor commented simply, "Well, now Ray knows."

I don't know what I expected—maybe some quote from Revelation explaining the answers in minute detail. Glimpses of answers to both questions can be found, but Wideman's short answer reiterated that none of us human beings will know the mind of God until we meet Him face to face.

Some grieving friends have told me, "I've had conversations with my loved one at graveside in the days and weeks following burial." Who am I to say that the Holy Spirit does not allow such interchanges to take place? Though nothing like this has been my personal experience, whatever helps each of us walk through the deep hurt of grief is probably okay with God. It's doubtful any of us realize the infiniteness of our God. He is the only One who knows exactly what our choices, decisions and future will be.

Dear God, increase my faith to acknowledge that You are all-seeing, all-knowing and ever-present. Amen

Do the Scars Ever Heal?

And this same God who takes care of me will supply all your needs . . .
Philippians 4:19 (NLT)

Are you, like me, wearing scars others cannot see? Not the scars from running barefoot over a piece of broken glass or falling down the stairs. Not even the kind of scars that required stitches.

I'm talking about the scars you and I acquired by losing someone we dearly loved. Some days these scars feel larger than others. Sometimes it feels as if the hole comes straight from my heart. Other times, I feel like I'm living a life that has been ripped in half.

I've read that scar tissue is stronger than ordinary tissue. If that is true, why don't you and I feel stronger? Others often say the wound will heal over time. My friend, Sharon, has an ulcer on her leg that never completely heals. She must use special medications and wear a specific kind of stocking bandage at all times. She has learned to live with it, but she knows she must take care.

Perhaps that is how it will be for us. We will learn to live with the scars from the loss of our loved one, but we must take care of ourselves. My taking care today? I'll get up, make my bed, shower, get dressed and eat nutritious food.

> *Dear God, my scars are wretchedly painful today.*
> *Allow me to focus on taking care of myself. Amen.*

Taking care of myself focus today _____

_____

_____

_____

_____

_____

_____

_____

One Foot in Front of the Other

I love you, Lord; you are my strength. Psalm 18:1 (NLT)

Although Jennifer Rothschild's blog had nothing to do with grief, the question in the blog title read, "How do you get through what you can't get over?"

I have found this question so appropriate. Whether it's been eight days, eight years or twenty- eight years, the death of my loved one is an occurrence I may never get over. But it has been a part of my life I am currently walking and have walked through.

Those first days and months, I just existed in emotional pain. My circle of family and friends helped. They sat with me, waited on me, took me places. Others told me later they did not know what to do so they stayed away for a time. These became my new normal circumstances.

I forced myself to write down two or three blessings each day and read them over as days came and went. I spent time reminding myself that Don would never again have pain, struggles or problems. At times, I visualized him worshipping with love at Jesus' feet. That image helped.

How did I get through those first most difficult weeks? I forced myself to some regular schedule of living. For me that schedule meant returning to work, returning to church and doing normal activities: getting the car serviced; going to the bank; buying some groceries. One friend, who had lost his wife the previous year described it this way, "Put one foot in front of the other and keep on walking."

Encouraging Words: Sadness is overwhelming emotional pain. Though it's invisible to those around us, God can and will give each of us the strength to move ahead. Amen.

Celebrate the Holiday?

"Glory to God in the highest heaven, and peace on earth to all whom God favors."
Luke 2:14 (NLT)

How will you make it through the holidays? Every ornament, every twinkling light, every festive wreath, every church service will be constant reminders of who is not there to enjoy these times with you. What must you do to get through these days? Do something very different than before.

Your family will not do this the way my family managed to approach the holidays. Perhaps you will find some commonalities that will be blessings during your struggle.

Christmas Eve had always started with attending candlelight service at six o'clock followed by soups, sandwiches and Christmas pie. Gifts were opened with extended family. Christmas morning cinnamon rolls always had a birthday candle in them to accompany our singing of "Happy Birthday, Jesus." Traveling to Christmas dinner with family and friends filled the entire day.

How did we make it through that first Christmas? My son, daughter-in-law, their son and daughter invited my daughter and her family, both grandmothers, and me for Christmas Eve. We traveled the two hours to their home, ate an entirely different menu than had been our tradition, read the Luke 2 Scripture, opened gifts, put on pajamas and retreated to their family room to watch Christmas movies until we became too drowsy to stay awake. Our holiday was accomplished with minimal tears.

Dear God, the joy of the season honors You, even when we are extremely sad.
A change of venue most definitely helps. Amen.

Don't Quit ... Persevere

As you know, we consider blessed those who have persevered...the Lord is full of compassion and mercy. James 5:11-12 (NIV)

Are you feeling God is distant today? What might you do to feel closer to him?

Some days I walk in the woods near my neighborhood. A walk by the lake soothed me one day. On several days, it was a walk with a friend at a nearby park. Without realizing it at the time, they all pointed me back to God.

One day I sensed God whispering, "Sorry for any inconvenience grief causes, but please don't give up. I'm writing a section of your life story that needs to be shared."

If God is whispering that same thing to you, you might be saying, "I do not want my life story written like this."

If you are like me, you may be yelling in silence between sobs, "I never intended to be a widow at my age. I planned to be a little white-haired lady riding beside a tall white-haired man in a vintage Ford Mustang convertible."

It's interesting how I planned my personal timeline for what I thought God should do in my life. He may have rolled His eyes because He always sees the whole picture. Over and over again, I've heard God's quiet voice saying, "Don't quit. Persevere."

So, I encourage you as I do myself, "Don't quit. Persevere." God is writing both of our life stories so that others may read them and see Him.

Dear Lord, if I'm honest, I do not want to be a quitter.
I'll thank You through my tears if You can use even a bit of what is
happening to me as cause for others to see You. Amen

God's Timing with Comfort

The memory of the righteous shall be a blessing. Proverbs 10:7 (NIV)

The Sunday before Christmas, my friend, Cheryl, tucked a gift in the pocket of my blazer.

After the holiday, I realized I had never opened it. On my next trip to my son's home, my daughter-in-law remarked, "You know there's a small Christmas gift in the room where you slept."

On top of the chest sat a partially obscured box. I hurriedly opened it. There it was—a Hallmark ornament—containing Don's photo and the following words, "When a stone is dropped into a lake, it quickly disappears from sight—but its impact leaves behind a series of ripples that broaden and reach across the water. In the same way, the impact of one life lived for Christ will leave behind an influence for good that will reach the lives of many others." Roy Lessin,[2] the author of these words never knew any of our family. But his words have brought comfort to me every time I've read them. Perhaps they will do the same for you.

I won't tell you there were no tears because they often appeared. God's timing was so excellent. He knew I could not handle this precious memory gift at the time it was given. It had to be opened later.

Dear God, thank you for precious friends who remember
in meaningful ways. Amen.

Remembrances of comfort _____

_____

_____

_____

_____

_____

_____

The Effort of Sadness

My spirit is broken... Job 17:1 (NIV)

After the funeral, how do you go back to the routine of daily life?

I wanted to scream, "My loved one died. Does anyone truly care?" I have to think most likely they did care, but the pace of their lives resumed. My life, as yours, changed forever.

Our God is a gracious, good God. But one minute I was overwhelmed, one minute I was angry and the next minute I just felt so empty. Every habitual thing was an effort. I made myself shower. I forced myself to eat. And when I lay down to sleep, I simply wanted to wake up with everything being all right. I wanted to just sleep–if I could get to sleep–because I wanted the hurt to go away. After my husband's death, my pillow survived many tears.

God showed His presence and comfort through dearest friends and my church family as they let me be myself. Their words and actions were reminders of hope when I needed it most.

Dear God, thank you that You used others to hold my hand. Thank you for this
help during a heart-wrenching time. Thank You for giving Your only Son on the
cross so believers are assured of spending eternity with You.
Continue to help me see blessings of each day. Amen.

Hope and blessings found _____

_____

_____

_____

_____

_____

_____

God Allows Suffering

But as for me, I know that my Redeemer lives, and that he will stand.
Job 19:25a (NLT)

In the case of my family and me, a life was cut short before its time. My children's dad, my husband, had retirement planned for some future date.

The story of Job showed me that even those who live uprightly may experience suffering that will not be understood in this lifetime. I have felt this truth before at other deaths–after a lengthy illness or untimely and sudden tragedy. Even with the compassion I had felt for others, surely 'no one else has ever endured this pain I felt.

I've learned not to judge how anyone chooses to grieve. Each of us have our own ways. For a whole year, my son listened to a CD of his Dad's funeral every time he mowed his yard. My daughter exclaimed, "Sometimes I just want to call God on the phone and say, 'I want to talk to my Dad about something.'"

The story of Job, shows us that God permits suffering, even when it is not deserved. He chooses to allow it in different ways. In our family's case, cancer ravaged the athletic body of my husband. Then we all learned how to grieve.

Oh Lord, give me this day again the realization that You do allow suffering in this life. We will never understand it while we live on earth. Amen.

Suffering not understood _____

_____

_____

_____

_____

_____

_____

_____

Replace the Why

God did not send his Son into the world to condemn it, but to save it.
John 3:17(NLT)

"I prayed for healing. Why didn't it happen?"

During my angry times of grieving, this question was the one I most often thought. Perhaps your grief is brought on by the lengthy illness of your loved one. Or you may be asking, "Why did this accident happen? Why did I have no warning? Why, why, why?"

Whatever your grieving self may be asking, it is normal and okay. From the time we are born, we are preparing for death. The joyous knowledge that the one I loved was a Christian and is in heaven does not replace any of the hurt. I know it should.

What has helped me most? God never promised total healing or lack of pain on this earth.

What He did promise is life eternal with Him if we ask to be forgiven of our sins and invite Him to live in our hearts and lives forever.

My pastor may have said it best when he remarked, "Sometimes a person's life speaks even more for Christ after he dies than when he was living." If this is true in your situation, I hope you will be comforted today.

Encouraging Words: God gives eternal life when He is invited into our hearts and lives. Help us to replace the whys of grief with this promise of God.

God's promise to accept _____

_____

_____

Finding Joy in Grief

Oh Lord, my God, how great you are! When you send your Spirit,
new life is born.... Psalm 104:1b and Psalm 104:30a (NLT)

A week after the funeral, my friend Sandy came by and insisted, "Let's go for a walk." "What's going on?" she asked, "What do you need?"

"I just want to find joy in living," I responded.

As we walked up and down the hills of my neighborhood, she pointed out the beauty of roses and other flowers. She reminded me of the magnificent trees that stood serenely by. "Listen," she continued, "a puppy is barking to be recognized, a bird sings when it doesn't care if anyone is listening, a squirrel scampers up the nearest tree to find his home. Life is about living no matter what our situation may be."

Sandy showed me what I needed most was to know someone cared, someone had not forgotten. At the time, I thought I needed sympathy. What I really needed was for someone to point out the blessings of life that I simply could not see. What I didn't need was to be told, "Everything will be all right."

For those of us experiencing grief, life will never be the same. However, I found comfort by observing nature, by being listened to, and being allowed to talk about my pain.

Later, I found comfort by reading Psalms. It was so hard to concentrate, it seemed almost impossible to read anything. But I persevered.

Psalm 104 mentions giving thanks for stars, for rain clouds, for wind, for mountains, for thunder, for animals, for birds, for food, for trees, for rocks. Then it concludes by telling us to rejoice in the Lord.

Encouraging Words: Friends show us that the one we are grieving has not been forgotten. Those friends can listen, walk with us and be Psalms with skin on. We must let them.

Joys to be found _____

_____

_____

_____

_____

_____

_____

_____

_____

No Right or Wrong

We do not know what to do but we are looking to you for help.
2 Chronicles 20:12b (NLT)

Have you noticed things seem worse when you are by yourself and it is late at night? I found this happening numerous times during the year(s) after I'd buried my husband. Friends suggested, "Get up and read a book. Watch TV. Work on an unfinished project."

My experience was that I could not do any of the suggestions more than twenty minutes.

Why? My attention span was simply too short. What seemed easier to me was to walk through the house, sit in a favorite chair and remember: details of the death's cause, details of the funeral, details of so many times spent together. Sometimes I sat and stared. Sometimes I sobbed quietly. Sometimes I pounded my fist on the chair arm.

I learned without being told, there is no right or wrong way to grieve.

I kept trying to remember God's love had not changed just because my life had been turned upside down. Finally, I found some peace when I clasped my hands together, hugged myself, and centered my thoughts to focus on the all-knowing, all-seeing Master of the Universe. Most of the time, I was able to walk back to my bed knowing the help I had been looking for was close at hand.

Dear God, it's not wrong to have deep feelings for those we have loved.
Allow me to accept Your help--to rest in You. Amen.

Ways to grieve_____

_____

_____

_____

_____

_____

From the Darkness

Even though I walk through the valley of the shadow of death, I fear no evil;
for Thou art with me. Psalm 23:4a (NASB)

"When I pass through deep waters, I paddle with poetry," remarks Jon Hopkins when he speaks about writing from the darkness of grief. He says, "When I can't sleep in the middle of the night, I simply write." He speaks from his years of experience after becoming a widower. He contends that the darkness has sometimes been times of intense grief due to death, Other times, the grief is due to circumstances–loss of a job, loss of a house, loss of a friend or family member due to drug overdose. One of his poems follows:

Deep Grace

What joys are born from earthly sorrows,

And the fear hearts bear of gloomy tomorrows?

With toils and drudgery that break hope's walls

And truths believed that brought us falls?

Apprehension, Wishes, Desires to end

A life overwhelmed, unwilling to bend

How much can one do without breaking down

When grieving destroys love's fragile crown?

Told to have strength, offered prayers of great peace

Sin remembered and a desire for release.

Help faintly bidden, Suspicions ruled out,

We give up our hope and no longer shout.

Quiet words of desperation and a need to be free;

We choose the path that only we can see.

The questions remain how we even arrived

And God in His plan found to save us alive.

Oft times we're sent angels through doubt and despair

To remind us of truths that God is still there.

So, hold tight to His hand and let not sorrow erase
These hard trudges with Him through times of deep grace.

Dear Lord, the mystery of your grace-filled comfort is unbelievable. Amen

Thoughts from the darkness _____

_____

_____

_____

_____

Who You Want Me to Be

We know that in all things God works for good for those who love him, for those whom he has called according to his purpose. Romans 8:28 (NIV)

Although much time has passed since the death of my husband, sometimes the emotional hurt still hurts. Memories of when I could have been nicer to my husband, more understanding, more considerate haunt my thoughts.

Why do I remember saying words that hurt, "What I think you should do is ...?" Why do I remember, "I don't want to ...?"

Within my hurt, I force myself to think. I've been a Christian a long time. Every day I've prayed for God to make me who He wants me to be. Could my questioning, my suggestions, simply have been part of our long-term relationship and may have been what was needed at the time? The Holy Spirit reminds me that time after time.

The Holy Spirit reminds me time after time, I prayed, "Lord make Don into the person you want him to be, because if he's made into the person I want him to be—he can never become who You want him to be."

What if I had never allowed myself to love? Maybe it would hurt less now. Would I ever want to throw away the wonderful times we shared? I would not.

In the quietness of these moments I spend with God, I do this remembering. Suddenly, I'm joyful. No, life will never be the same, but I still must be thankful.

Dear God, bring joy to my life as I thank you for experiences and memories shared with the one I loved. Amen

Jesus Cares Enough

Then Jesus wept. John 11:35 (NLT)

Have you ever been in a church gathering when a favorite Scripture verse was requested?

Both children and adults have blurted out, "Jesus wept."

Sometimes neither the younger nor the older have been aware of the reason for Jesus' tears. Have you ever researched what was really happening in John 11? My friend, Jeanette, says Jesus joined the mourners knowing he could raise his friend, Lazarus, from the dead.

I know God can heal. I just don't know why He chooses to heal some and allows others to go without healing on this earth. Jeanette suggests Jesus might have wept out of sympathy and love. Perhaps He wept, because life can be cruel and death inevitable for all who are human. Still, Jeanette said, "Jesus cared enough to weep."

She continued, "When we deal with difficult situations or experience grief, Jesus understands."

Then she added the most profound statement I heard in my first days of grief, "God may not always stop the funeral, but he'll always weep with us."

Dear God, my current situation is reducing me to tears again today. Your presence is here with me even when, humanly, I can't feel it. Amen.

Heaven is Closer

"I, the Son of God will receive glory from this." John 11:4b (NLT)

Have you thought that heaven is closer now because someone's soul we know resides there?

John 11 tells the story of Jesus coming to His dear friends' house. Mary and Martha were grieving deeply because their brother, Lazarus had died.

When Martha heard Jesus was on his way, she rushed down the road to meet him. She exclaimed, "Lord, if you had been here, my brother would not have died."

I wonder why these were her words? She could have said, "Thank you for coming. My brother loved you so much."

Then Scripture tells that Martha pulled Mary aside from those who were at their home trying to console them. She said, "The Teacher is here and wants to see you." Mary immediately went to him.

After she fell down at his feet, the first thing Mary said was, "Lord, if you had been here, my brother would not have died." Isn't it interesting they both told Jesus the same words?

Jesus responded, "Didn't I tell you that you will see God's glory if you believe?"

You and I do not feel any better that our friend, Jesus, has not physically arrived at our front door.

My former pastor, Tiger Pennington, explained it this way at an Easter Sunday service, "Jesus can deliver. He comes to bring the future of heaven into the present. He didn't come to show up for death. He came to bring life."

What a promise. Jesus has purpose for you and me even when we are saddest. Heaven definitely feels closer than it ever has been.

Dear God, In this, my saddest hour, thank you for the promise of purpose.
Heaven does seem closer now. Amen.

How does Heaven seem closer or does it?_____

_____

_____

_____

_____

_____

_____

_____

_____

_____

Me–Ask for Help?
The Lord is good, a refuge in times of trouble.
He cares for those who trust in him. Nahum 1:7 (NIV)

"Stop, my loved one died. My life has wanted to scream."

Has this thought crossed your mind at least once? For me, friends and neighbors returned quickly to the busyness of their lives. I never screamed it, but I felt I had every right to. It is true, I think, that most of us postpone thoughts about death until it slaps us in the face.

Some came to me and simply said, "I care." Some happened to be Christian friends who had navigated the days, months, and years after losing someone close to them.

I asked, "How did you make it?" Not everything I heard applied to me–but I did listen. God uses others who have been in our same situation to shed light on our needs.

If you don't have anyone to listen or ask these questions, I will listen. Email me at zetadavidson@gmail.com.

Another great help is to Google GriefShare[3] on your phone or computer. GriefShare offers faith-based classes to help you journey through the dark days and nights ahead. I found the first couple of classes to be difficult to sit through. I was forced to confront my new reality. By the third of the eighteen weeks of classes, I learned so many of my emotions and feelings were natural. I wasn't going crazy after all. Each of us can journey through this time at our own speed and in our own way.

Consulting with my attorney became a wise thing to do, even though there was a will and trust and joint property. It was not a time for my primary care physician to become a stranger. I needed medication. I found my way when I didn't want to–realizing I had not passed this way before.

Dear Lord, show me how to handle this grief that seems
not so understandable. Amen.

Show me how to reach out for help. Amen.

Feeling and emotions the same or different from before someone so close died?

_____

_____

_____

_____

Tips from Christian friends on "How did you make it?"

_____

_____

_____

_____

Notes from GriefShare[3] website:

_____

_____

_____

_____

Attorney's address, phone and email:

_____

_____

Primary care physician's address, phone and email:

_____

_____

Help Others? Me?

Here on earth you will have many trials and sorrows. But take heart, because I have overcome the world. John 16:33b (NLT)

"I know exactly how you feel." Without a doubt, someone has voiced that to you.

It's not that anyone else's loved one has never died. The newspaper obituary columns are filled day after day. In fact, I looked at my husband's photo and read and reread his announcement time after time. It was one way of convincing myself that he was not coming back.

Death had never happened to someone I was so close to. I had not realized—as one friend said, "I feel like my right arm has been torn off."

What wouldn't I give for just one more time to say, "I love you?" Of course, I really don't know, but I remember thinking there would never be that chance.

No one knows exactly how you feel. I don't. And anyone who says this can never know how you or I feel.

More than once I pounded my pillow—yes, the one damp with tears. I did finally learn that feelings are just that—feelings. It's okay to feel any way a person wants to while grieving. For my own health, through grief classes, I learned it is not okay to stay stuck in the depths of despair. I learned to get up and do the next thing there is to do.

In retrospect, what helped me most was to find someone else to help—someone who was worse off than me. You may be saying, "I don't want to do that." I did it anyway and found helping another helped me.

Dear God, thank you for allowing the closest of relationships between human beings. Show each of us how to help others. Amen

Describe your reaction when someone said, "I know exactly how you feel."

_____

_____

_____

_____

_____

_____

_____

_____

_____

_____

What is your plan to not get stuck in grief? _____

_____

_____

_____

_____

_____

_____

Acknowledgements

Heather Beers for editing the rough draft. Sandra Skaggs for reading the edited manuscript.

Cathy Gibbons Reedy for book and cover design.

RJ Thesman for editing the final manuscript and for being my excellent writing coach.

Heart of America Christian Writers Network for membership, conferences and continuing encouragement.

Thank you to every person mentioned in this book who lived this grief experience with me, especially my 100-year-old mother, Velda Combs, and my immediate family, Jay and Anne Davidson, Ryann and Will Davidson, Bart and Paige Davidson Price, Cooper, Carter and Cailyn Price.

About the Author

An award-winning author, Zeta Combs Davidson, has been published in *Standard, Metro Voice News, Living with Children, Home Life and Deacon Magazine.* Her work has been featured in *Guideposts' Divine Interventions-Heartwarming Stories of Answered Prayer, A Cup of Comfort-Devotionals for Mothers, The Gift of Prayer, Living the Serenity Prayer, The Best Advice I Ever Got, Love is a Flame, Love is a Verb, I'll Be Home for Christmas, 101 Facets of Faith and MOPS' A Comet's Tail-Mentoring-Wisdom to Light the Way.*

In addition to having taught more than 2500 juniors and seniors in Marriage and Family Living in public high school, Zeta speaks to Christian women across Kansas and Missouri.

She serves on the board of the Women's Ministry Missouri Baptist Children's Home, teaches women's Bible studies and is an Ambassador in Guest Services at North Kansas City Hospital.

Zeta holds both Bachelor's and Master's degrees in Family Life Education. She has been selected for Who's Who of American Women and Who's Who of American Educators.

She serves as Membership Director on the board of Heart of American Christian Writers Network. Meeting Moments and Market Leads are two articles she writes monthly for *The Write Connection* newsletter emailed to HACWN membership.

Zeta grew up on a dairy farm in Gentry County, MO and is the mother of two and grandmother of five.

After being a widow for thirteen years, Zeta wrote *Strength for the Sadness* to encourage God's work and His blessings in ordinary lives.

Endnotes

1 Max Lucado. Nashville, TN (Thomas Nelson Publishers). *You'll Get Through This: Hope and Help for Your Turbulent Times. Sept. 2013.*

2 Roy Lessin. https://grateful-for-life.blogspot.com/2009/10/impact-of-one-life.html. Also found on DaySpring Cards ornament. 2007.

3 https://www.griefshare.org. GriefShare. PO Box 1739. Wake Forest, NC. 27588-1739.

CPSIA information can be obtained
at www.ICGtesting.com
Printed in the USA
LVHW012334061020
668070LV00008B/525